A Pilgrim into Silence

Other books by Karen Swenson

An Attic of Ideals (Doubleday, 1967)

A Sense of Direction (Smith Press, 1989)

The Landlady in Bangkok (Copper Canyon, 1994)

A Daughter's Latitude (Copper Canyon, 1999)

A Pilgrim into Silence

Poems

Karen Swenson

For my former roommates on their journey toward the perfect apartment Love to George + Gloria from, Karen 4/15/11

Tiger Bark Press • Rochester, New York • 2008

Published by Tiger Bark Press,
479 Ravenwood Ave., Rochester, NY 14619.

Cover design by Jana Brenning.

Cover photography by the author.

Text design by Philip Memmer.

ISBN: 978-0-9816752-0-6

Acknowledgements

Commonweal: "What Woman Has a Country?," " Why I Went to Mother Teresa's," "The Voyeurs";
Juniate Voices: "The Cultural Bigamist," retitled " Bigamy";
Literary Imagination: "Mardi Gras";
Luna: "The Anglo-Indian";
Pivot: "What Is Broken";
Poetry London: "The Silence of the Birds;" "Morticians, New York City;" "The Crow, Calcutta";
Poetry New Zealand: "How Many Mothers?";
Prairie Schooner: "Without Reservations," "The Dog Tooth of Faith," "The Blind Dog of Hope," "The Coin," "Two Recovered," "The Burning Ghat," "At Mother Teresa's," "Two Foreign Volunteers," "The Thief," "Saintly Success," "Fifth Avenue," "An Obit of Crows for the Dorset Hotel," retitled "The Crows' Obituary for the Dorset Hotel," "Epiphany in a Tent";
Rattapallax: "Femme Fatale";
Runes: "Sweet Reveille on 54th St.";
Salmagundi: "The Phantom at the Opera," "No More";
Southwest Review: "Rats in Lhasa," "Sparrows";
Square One: "A Pilgrim Into Silence";
The Little Magazine: "There Is No Good Without Its Attendant Evil";
Weber Studies: "A Neighbor";
Yale Review: "Thanksgiving";

Anthologies

AnthologY: Visiting Authors, 2006: "232 Faringdon Rd.;" "Gypsy;" "Layle Silbert";
Conversation Pieces: poems that talk to other poems: "A Girl Goes Into the World";
Poetry in Performance 30: "Transparent Girl";
Poetry in Performance 32: "Circumambulating Mount Kailash";

CONTENTS

HOME

This book is fondly dedicated to
Marie Ponsot, Daryl Chinn, and Estha Lynne Weiner,
whose suggestions and commentary were so often met
with stiff-necked resistance.

Copious thanks to the Lannan Foundation,
which gave me two months of writing time
at their extraordinary colony in lovely Marfa, Texas.

Thanksgiving

THANKSGIVING

The Thanksgiving after Mother's death, believing
in the landscaped shade of tradition there'd be safety,
I drove with my son to the green-lawned suburb of Death
my mother had moved her marriage to, a well
decored edition of the anteroom
I've seen in Nepal near burning *ghats* along
the Bagmati River. The old, belongings knotted
in scraps of cloth set neatly on their cots,
eat, watch the neighbors' ashes float downstream
and wait their turn. But in the Connecticut
version, with walk-in closets plus dishwasher,
my father survived on vodka and frozen dinners.

A fragrance of turkey, duck a bonus, welcomed
us to memory's censored holidays, from which
all ill and anger were erased. My father,
a belt of vodka in the kitchen with
each plate he brought to table, first glowed at
our praise, then gloomed through turkey ribs, then
glowered at the duck carcass, metamorphosis
complete from Party Prince to Goblin as
he aimed a duck thigh at his grandson, yelling
with each throw, accurate as a winning dart,
"You take it all. You don't leave anything.
There's nothing left. There's nothing left for me."

My son on the bus back to the city, I returned
to placid snores, my father passed out behind
his bedroom door. I drank myself to sleep.
By that bizarre entente between all drunks,
the morning brought no mention of the night.
Boys in the brown Bagmati, sleek
as rain-wet leaves, swim, plummet, cannonball

among the wind-light powder of life, gray-down
that takes the current watched by the old, without
walk-in closets or dishwashers, just
a clutch of moments, yellow *kafel* berries,
a handful, ripe and warm in an open palm.

POP

Pop goes the weasel. Pop, I named him knowing
he wanted to be Dad, a two year old
arranging her small kingdom of control.
Already headed out, the bottle towing
him beyond restraint, to the alcoholic current,
a rip-tide taking him from his wife, his life
and me on a lonely voyage through seas rife
with deep monsters, fears from the bottle's content,
climbing up the ship's side, tentacles slimy
and sucking. We could see him battling air
until at last his sail fell behind the filmy
horizon. I loved him as you love in despair
a sailor lost at sea, setting up an easel
to paint from memory. Pop goes the weasel.

ACCUSED

When my son boycotts me at Christmas, I
know I'm accused, charges undisclosed,
a blanket indictment—which I smuggled
into the garbage, stained, rank, shredded. But
it's arraignments of the self without a plea
that lead to the penal servitude of guilt.
Not slaps and yells, but the mother, muffled in
a stale swaddle of beer, who, appearing present,
was untouchable, a figment of the bottle's
imagination. I serve the sentence of
a woman dead now twenty years, trying
to rehabilitate the touch ungiven, lost
as the perfume of my baby's milky mouth,
to give my presence too late in the season.

THE SHADE

—*For Ashley Mace Havird*

A shade of shades, beneath a shepherdess
lamp hooded in a flute of pastel silk,
she was a fragrance of face powder whose
pink dusted her well-buttressed bosom, caulked
cheeks pleated as a summer fan fluttering
one wing in a liver-spotted hand.
Silk tasseled cords pulled blinds against the sun
where I in first, and she approaching second,
childhood played at poker, betting matchsticks,
while sipping from translucent robin-egg cups,
the milky, cambric tea I was allowed.
This neighbor's white head—pale moon, fading into
the daylight's bright among crocheted mats, her china
birds, ivory elephants was chatelaine
of my dream home filled with mysterious foreign objects
where I was loved
                              because I was a girl.

BEAUTY

The son of a friend of my mother's he,
to my humiliation, was called when
I couldn't produce a date for the St. Nick Ball.
Two years my senior he'd filibuster
me on life, driving home through
decorous and dark suburban streets. Dead trees alive
with lights glowed in the windows. Once he said,
"Those men are fools who marry pretty girls
and beautiful is worse. They'll be unfaithful.
A homely girl will feel beholden to
her husband. He chose her when no one would."

My mother wrote me ten years later. "Rick's
bride is the homeliest girl that you ever,
but practical, a major in accounting."

And I? I found a Greek coin, an Adonis
with dark curls and wine deep eyes. Walking into
a party, we weren't a pair. At his face
a room went still as a river pool before
white water. I became invisible
as Beauty's precedence obliterated me.
It's true, he wasn't faithful, yet, until
it hurt too much, I lived with that ineffable,
which, when translated flesh to stone,
becomes a member of the numinous—
a crowd it's always been a risk to sleep with.

SPARROWS

Small, cute, as Nemerov notes, they, unlike
the tiger, freely hop between bars in
exchange for picking seeds from shit. They are
the common-people bird, the universal
UN family of small wings, which
in Bangkok gutters peck spilled rice or roost
between spines on catclaw cactus in
Chihuahua's desert. Quarrelsome in spring on
my city terrace, they puff and ruffle up
to macho feather-balls against the finches.
But come a warm June evening, rancor gone,
brown pinstripes smooth, one holds the rail, his soft
throat-feathers pulsing song, just as my wrist
beats my blood, in the mindlessness of beauty.

FEMME FATALE

—For Khay Cochran (1926-2000)

A little succession of railcars;
a titled marriage, St. Louis-Paris,
the caboose divorce.
Depositing the child with her banker parents,
she sailed to erase, with the right friends and fashions,
her humiliation, that her body could be used
by powers stronger than her will.
The father was forced, in the divorce, to sign
his son away who remembers being in
her company for, maybe, seventy-two
hours in his life that now has as many years.

What he remembers, outside of family gossip,
of her Parisian life and elite loves, is
her walking toward him, his mother, through a green
sway of wheat, her skirt flickered by the dusty
tongue of a summer breeze. The sun in the parting
of her red hair struck a dazzle, anointed her
with a diamond blaze, a moment's light.

MARDI GRAS

Dried out, an old robe hung up damply over
a balcony rail, she'll stay sober
some years, then her old fantasies of life
still strong at 80, rented costumes
for Mardi Gras—she thinks life is, or should
be, Mardi Gras before the Lent of Death—
begin to glow in her closet. Masquerades
of three-inch heels with ankle straps,
chipped bugle beads, frayed feathers hold
a bouquet of stale sweat.

          All shimmer, they
don't suit the wife whose husband charmed the college
girl next door to bed,
the woman who sewed seams to order
whose daughter lives in Santa Fe
with a drunken bluegrass fiddler.

          Alone,
one room, a bow of balcony,
enough for one chair, table and the orchids
that raise fantasticated heads
in lavenders, greens, and bronzes to the nurture
of her hands, which pluck this afternoon
an elegant, long-stemmed glass from the shelf,
fill it with white wine.

          On her terrace,
the lady, elegant as her glass, has—
legs knowledgeably crossed to flash
her ankle straps—a little sip of wine
a little sip, a little ….

THE PHANTOM AT THE OPERA

Above the aria I scent her
cadaver reek, alcohol seepage
through perfumed pores. I know that smell,
familiar of my soul. As Violetta
sings with TB lungs of love,
this stranger in the dark, gold at her fingers
and ears, perfect cherry-lacquered nails,
is an unaccompanied decomposition
conducted by gin through scene after scene—
pint tangled with her stockings in her drawer,
the furtive slug of cooking sherry
or the gulp from the bottle in her purse.
Germont sings his duet with Violetta,
but I hear my neighbor's aria with fear,
recalling each tremolo, inhaling my
own bottle-dread real as breath, and she's
its specter next to me.
At intermission she leaves in her mink, but
I know the score. While Violetta has
her last ecstatic moments, my ghost, home
alone, holds her pose before her claque of empties.

A NEIGHBOR

Gray as Tenth Avenue hotel sheets,
she unflaps her cardboard-carton house perched
on a vacant townhouse stoop,
feels layers of her laundry cart
parked on the sidewalk under plastic
tucked like a shower cap.
With the precision of a woman
who knows her gold bracelet
is packed in the throat of her
black turtleneck, she pulls
out her cosmetic case
of silver vinyl. Over last
night's coat of diesel grime,
she applies today's foundation,
parting, with a sideways glance,
her mascara-stuck lashes. Passing men
may pity. Women know the face
fractured in her shard of mirror.

NO MORE

No more for me the honey or the sting;
let others, hungry for those sweet cells, risk
the pain. I thought, I'll school my appetite
to safer nourishment and not go ailing—
my venom-stung heart swollen to a fist.
Nor did I live on lemon peels of spite
through those years, though perhaps a little blandly.
But here you come, a deadly pollen count,
reeking lavender and clover, voice
thick with the hive's wild thrumming melody.
Lips sticky from those nectared chambers mount
mine, urge, delectably, against my choice.
    In sting-proof clothing, I frown from the shadow
    of protective veils; you waltz the wildflower meadow.

TEHERAN, THE FOOD COURT

Like pigeons winging down on a spill of breadcrumbs
they flutter, headscarves loose over hair black as lacquer.
Authority—of heaven or earth—succumbs
to hormones, kohl lined eyes without rancor.
In wallpaper tight jeans and hip-length jackets so snug
the fabric stretches to parentheses
between the buttons, they giggle across tables and mug
for each others' cameras in the greasy sleaze
of make-believe foreign restaurants, even
a Tex-Mex. An isle of adolescent liberty,
where boys stroll by to look at faces that leaven
dreams, creating divine and political difficulty.
The essence of adolescence is invariably heathen
and totally in opposition to religion and reason.

NEW YORK MORTICIANS

These city cousins of the roadside
morticians of America,
consumers of car-kill on country
routes, strutted their oil-slick sleek feathers
on the 14th floor terrace railings
of the abandoned hotel across the street.

The three black cynics cawing wisecracks
down at the stream of yellow taxis
have been a seasonal constant whether
as shadows winging through snow or
a darkness knifing through skyscraped
shards of August sun,
until this summer's Nile fever laid
soft-bodied sparrows and finches on sidewalks.

Now there are two left, mourners doing
the side-step shuffle along the length
of terrace rail, then lifting off
in their patrol above the green
park for mates to make up the loss.

At Mother Teresa's in Calcutta

In 1998 I worked for a month at Mother Teresa's Home
for the Dying Destitute in Calcutta. These poems attempt
to encapsulate the experience of working in that hospice
where women and men lay in separate sections dying,
undiagnosed and largely without medicine.
The Home is next to the most important Kali temple
in Calcutta, where hundreds of goats are daily sacrificed
in a ritual that, as any Calcutta taxi driver will attest,
guarantees that Kali, "a good mother," will take care of you.

THE CROW, CALCUTTA

Tea dregs, crumbs and white china creamer
set on the ledge of the open arch
that gazes down to starched red dahlias.
Along the ledge, on pogo-spring
legs, he bounds in a neat brown vest over
his plumage suit, sleek as a pair
of plastic patent leather shoes.
The artful city con man keeps
one jet eye on me as,
disdaining a banana skin,
tea leaves, and crumbs, he plunges his
blunt beak down to the bottom of
the china creamer. Head back, like
a woman laughing into her
arched neck, he savors the buttery, sapid
slide down his black throat, winks an onyx
eye at me in Calcutta sun.

WHY I WENT TO MOTHER TERESA'S

I'd watched three friends ensnared in wires and tubes,
their bodies fragile and imperfect among
white metal boxes blipping lights and beeps.
One danced his drug-induced hallucinations
in the embrace of clock-hands opposite
his bed. Another wept and pled with nurses
who forced a plastic tube down his gagging throat
because his daughter wasn't ready yet
to let him die. The third, among boxes
that hummed as if alive, lay still, her only
movement the sustained vibrato of her eyelids.
I wanted death stripped. Unobscured by its
décor of tubes and flashing disco lights, would
it terrify less, be more familiar naked?

AT MOTHER TERESA'S

Through the veil of skin I read bone's
lessons in braille, as the son
and daughter of Herr Mozart learned
their notes within the blindfold's dark.

Skin purses hold the small change of
malnourished life. I hear it clink
as I lift bodies bed to bath.

Each has her melody, carolling
behind life's blindfold, "I am, you
are, he/she/it, we, we are."
Bone syncopates, "Not long, not long."

TWO FOREIGN VOLUNTEERS

In rubber gloves we strip the beds,
some shitted yellow as the marigolds
which lei black Kali's neck. In Holland
a psychiatric nurse, here she's bemused,
as I am by how habit-forming
it is to wash the clothes and patients, their
skin crackled—sun-parched, river mud.
We shop, lunch with our fellow foreigners
on meat, not *dahl.* We move with ease
from the dead to the Oberoi Hotel,
at night watch Rambo videos
or else read Indian philosophy.
Returning in morning air, sour with exhaust,

we find a white-wrapped shape,
yesterday a face we knew, which waits
now to be carried to the *ghat.*
We hang green sheets and yellow-flowered gowns
to flap in sun above the stalls
adorned with Kali's pictures where she's
sticking out her tongue. The nurse
and I agree, it feels as if we almost
have a life here—a white-wrapped gift from Death.

THE CRY AT MOTHER TERESA'S

A first-day novice, stained sheet in one rubber
gloved hand, surrounded by the chaos
of nuns, patients, other foreigners, I thought,
"A baby? Where? Where is that baby crying,
in this place of the dying?" I saw, through
spaces of brick latticework set in
the wall, a patient, mouth agape in her
cry, cringing from cold water, soapy hands
of strangers on her nakedness. There was
no baby. No, it was nothing but all of us,
in the Calcutta morning maelstrom
of religion, the alien, death, strung upon
this moment's infinite umbilical—
a thin, high infant wail to emptiness.

THE COIN

They cannot speak; they do
not know, yet are each other.
Beneath dark caps of hair
they mirror other and self
across continents
and oceans. One thin through
commands of fashion. One
slimmed by intransigent
demands of her disease.
An elegance of cheek
bones, this pair of young faces
is—Indian, Italian—
obverse/reverse, head/tail
each of the alien other.
Like sisters they hold hands,
patient in Death's anteroom.

TWO RECOVERED

Excited, chattering, like sparrows in
a spring rain puddle, these two have grown well
among the dying. One so thin the tendons
on her arms protrude their rods. The other plump
and gray. They change from yellow-flowered nighties
to their own frayed and stained clothes as
if donning jewels and wedding wraps.
They, bending over each bed to say goodbye
to the dying, seem prepared for a distant journey
home. But there's no home, only sidewalk space
or the floor of Howrah Station on which to squat
among their fellow beggars. In two days
the plump one begs again at the hospice door,
freedom was a honeymoon of hunger.

THE AUSTRIAN

He's huge, a Western flesh-pile of chest and sinew,
with a voice redolent of elves and forests
on the Calcutta subway platform among
the sari butterflies and willow-wand men.

Since we share pallor in a brown world and
our working day among the dying, we
attempt a conversation. He asks,
"Terrible these people. You feel sorry?"

I say, "Yes," to keep us going, but no, not
pity, rather astonished admiration
for the sheer willfulness of life—a blind
and cornered cat slashing at Death's dogs.

THE THIEF

A stalking cat, she inches toward
the cubby full of foreigners'
strange treasure-stuff. This morning
she plucked hand cream from my pocket and
secreted it beneath her bed.
"No hidy-holes in this ward, Dear,"
I said and plucked it back. She reached to finger
my earrings, grinned without remorse.
The bug-eyed aide sees her now, yells,
a blue jay warning in a yard
at home— Cat! Cat! She scurries back
to bed, but as she turns I glimpse
the belly shape beneath her nightgown.
That's why she cleans her neighbors' tin
lunch plates. Perhaps sixteen, she winds,
unwinds the bandage on her hand.
I'll keep the belly's secret from
the celibate who take the young.

THE ANGLO-INDIAN

Half us, half them, she doesn't knit
us but makes us mutually
exclusive in her knot of pain
whose arms and legs cannot unfold.

Hers is a separate grief, an island
of malformed hand and foot, which speaks
two languages and leaves her heart,
a foreigner, mute in our midst.

She says grace for the nuns and her
uncomprehending fellows, has
a tantrum when we aliens
serve her tedious *dahl* and rice.

Her nightgown, white, not yellow like
the rest, is laundered separately
to fly next door to Kali's bloody
shrine, the pale banner of her difference.

THE BURNING *GHAT*

This young man, AIDS thin, yesterday hid from
our glances as we came to work. He tented
his blanket over razor-ridges of
his vertebrae, his shaved head, to reserve
a little privacy where he and Death
could confer. Today, alone in a cube
of wood and straw, he's flaming in a corner
of the *ghat*. No mourners. No son lit his pyre.
But Kali gazes, young and beautiful,
from an old stone fragment, beautiful as he was.

KALIGHAT IN CALCUTTA

The sheets and nightgowns semaphore a breeze,
next door to Kali's multicolored dome,
the sun-bleached, tattered signals from the dying.

Below, in the street, a mother suckles as
a barber shaves her head. We watch from where
the sheets and nightgowns semaphore a breeze.

Hair scatters under rickshaw wheels. Skull, breast,
child's head are brown balloons from here among
the sun-bleached, tattered signals from the dying.

Religion's sacrifice or lice? A sacred
cow breaks her fast on a shrine's marigolds,
while sheets and nightgowns semaphore a breeze.

A man, in the street's throbbing hive of color,
grills silver fish, sends up delicious incense
to sun-bleached, tattered signals from the dying.

Next door the gutters run with goat's blood, as Kali
imbibes her feast. Above those twitching legs,
the sun-bleached tattered signals from the dying
of sheets and nightgowns semaphore a breeze.

THERE IS NO GOOD
WITHOUT ITS ATTENDANT EVIL

If the number of the poor is reduced
we'll lose our jobs.
        —Sister Nirmala, Mother Teresa's successor.

It's a sort of deal:

On one side God controls
the bank, owns apple-blossom Heaven
and Hell's in-the-red embers;

while on the other, there's
an international, blue and
white wimpled corporation.

In the account between is the currency of the poor:

In yellow-flowered gowns—
unnamed but numbered—they'll wear
the amulet of any God who'll help.

Net profits on those savings are desirable:

Orphans and children of malnourished parents,
the cash flow of life,
are the dividends of redemption.

Deposits toward salvation may be made:

Circle death with beads of prayer;
sleep on concrete;
hold a patient's foot as
another cuts away the rotted skin
repeating sternly, "Be
still. Be still," to the asset
who's flinching from the pain.

SAINTLY SUCCESS

We think, outsiders to Heaven, that a saint,
perhaps, is someone whom love has led into
soul-alleys until lost in a purlieu
of goodness, or we sentimentally
suppose the saint is naturally glued
to "the good," a peanut-butter-jelly treat
of sticky sacred intimacy. But
at Mother Teresa's I thought good might be
an ambition—like making it as a movie star—
if you're a young, ambitious Albanian
girl born into a stifling closet—all
the world's doors locked but for marriage and the veil.
Good's lustrous portal out of suffocation
would lead, at least, to the open air of the world.

Tibet

I traveled to Tibet because of a promise I made to my dying aunt.
I have now gone there eight times, made friends with English
and without Tibetan and sometimes with no language at all.
Having a friend with whom speech is an impossibility
is a bond of spirit. I have lost a friend of ten years and tried
to tell her forbidden story. I have joined with other pilgrims
in circumambulating the holy mountain, Mt. Kailash,
sacred to Bonpos, Buddhists, Hindus, and Jains five times.
I have witnessed the aftermath of the Chinese destruction
of the Cultural Revolution, which left a desolate emptiness
that recently has been followed by the attempt to rebuild temples
for the tourist trade. Mao did not just destroy buildings in China
and Tibet, he tried, and largely succeeded in, denigrating
people's sense of, admiration of, love of, beauty.
The Chinese mocked the Tibetans for their fondness for flowers,
claiming it proved they were inferior, childish, and frivolous.

THE SILENCE OF THE BIRDS

—For Marie Ponsot

Mao ordered the Chinese to flap sheets and tarps in the fields
to keep the birds, which he believed ate too much grain,
in the air until they fell dead from exhaustion.

No sparrows in the streets of Chengdu fight
in dirty rain pools over spilled rice from foodstalls.
No pigeons murmur in the eaves of Du Fu's
government-rebuilt cottage. One grimy evening
above the River Jin's polluted current,
I watched a swallow scissoring solo, black
ghost of its dead brethren's silence who
with sparrows and mourning doves were forced to flight by
arms, tarps, sheets flapping until they plummeted,
small wings exhausted, hearts drummed out by Mao's
command. More slowly the remainder were dispatched
through DDT's expedience.

The only singing is in cages treasured
by old men in teahouses on the Jin's
trashed banks. The silence blanketing the fields
echoes from ribcages that centuries
have ruthlessly schooled to hood the heart's bird,
silence the soul's perilous lyrics.

WITHOUT RESERVATIONS

—For Elizabeth West (1887-1987)

Each visit we arranged her death, the list
of guests, new underclothes in tissue paper.
We sorted the instructions in the shoebox
her scrawl on scraps of paper, "Bury me,
no matter what the weather, in my pink
dress, pin the chiffon scarf with my blue brooch."

That Sunday, when I asked how she was, she
snapped like a screen door on its spring, "The way
you are at 99." I said, "Fine, but I'll
be furious with you if you die and
don't tell me." We laughed. In ten minutes she
called back, "Come. That is what is happening."

The shoebox done, in the Dakota kiln
of summer, with the fan at our feet turning
between us leisurely, we sat. She asked,
"There will be money. Where will you go when
I die?" The fan's breath flurried at my hem,
a murmur of moths. "Tibet." "Yes," she said.

The first stroke ate my name, the voices of many words.
She sat on the bed blowing
her nose on the top sheet as I arranged
for nurses. The next stroke came in September
while I taught. In October the home called
to say she had turned her face to the wall.

She would not eat or drink. "Tubes," they said. "No
tubes," I said. "Two days," they said. I looked
at her slides of Guatemala, riffled through
her guide to Luxor, booked a flight to Fargo
and knew I was an orphan. The scarf was pinned.
The guests invited. She left without reservations.

OFFERING

A black hat in a Sunday pew,
her silent aisle was circled by
the sea of sonorous hosannas.
Deaf to the sermon she was a blown
fuse in the spiritual circuit—
God to priest to the unordained souls.
In her, the sermon's vacancy,
its silence, was an empty bowl
open to the pouring of her
soul's voice. God answered back? From where?

Elsewhere.

I walk in darkness as yak butter
lamps shine in the blue eyes of gold-
cheeked Buddhas at
whose knees a row
of bowls present what anyone can give,
the sheen of water in a clean bowl.
We offer up what we've been given:
a bowl of water, a sermon's silence—
responses of transparency—
and God thrives upon our thirst.

HIMALAYA RAIN SHADOW

The mountain's green wall runs with rain.
It billows water-sails in wind
until each rock crack, each leaf vein
is murmuring refrains of water.

But over the pass the wind's whistle,
alone between white teeth of peaks
is keening a parched canticle
in wheeling oracles of dust.

If wet engenders leaves, then drought
is fertilizer of both spirit
and root to prodigies that grout
the rock with psalms of petals.

NIGHT

In night's plush dome of dark outside my tent
broadcast with stars, great, gaseous exhalations
of nebulae careering, I tilt my head
at Tibet's electric, fourteen thousand dry feet
to unfathomable dark where light, a current
flickering, is like the rumble from
a fanning hand on a taut drum skin.
Some astral tide takes me, all footing gone,
oars overboard. The rapids of darkness heave
me awestruck in tumult between the stars. I'm shrunk
to a flint-struck moment, to own my brevity,
a tittle of prattle, a cinder of inconsequence.
All seeds in my rainstick rattle to one end.
I lower my gaze and ego returns them again.

RATS IN LHASA

All over the rough sheet and pillowcase
their little charcoal nuggets of shit, plus
a strew across the floor as though a bored
child dribbled palmfuls of dark licorice.

I pull the chambermaid in to complain.
I point. She says, "You no here. They come. You
here. They no come." That comfort given, she
turns, a bright jangle of keys, out the door.

True. Sort of. Not one morrised on my bed,
but every morning their confetti witnessed
last night's fete through which I slept, though I tried
to keep my ears aware of nail and squeak.

As I sank into the wind's thin whistle through
a cracked pane, what anaudic tango, mute
waltz, muffled funky chicken, silently
caroused in Lhasa's cold beneath my bed?

WHAT IS BROKEN

To live with what is broken past glue or lies,
the cracked doll's head, the crumbled edge of clay,
the wrenched sheets of love's bed that symbolize
our bronze beliefs become papier-mache
is to hug tinseled fancies we idolize.

Both child and mother silently recognize
the hurts that never healed. Wrong's résumé
of scabs crust all we yearn to aphorize
in motherhood and childhood while we pray
to live with what is broken past glue or lies.

In different measure Tenzin Choedrack, eyes
gutted in the Chinese penance play
to empty cups of sockets, like the new pigsties
made from blasted monasteries, knows the way
is living with what's broken past glue or lies.

TASHI, 1936-2002

The cadre yanks the pearls from her neck, smiles
while spitting the acid reflux of contempt
into another's face. Still as dead water,
she listens to their rattle along the stone
floor, their lost leaps—ping, ping, ping, ping, ping, ping.
Lesson: Don't reach out to save anything.

In the Lhasa restaurant kitchen, body
shaking like a bridge beneath a truck's rumble,
she laughs into my shoulder, that sound of not
crying, never crying. Heads up quick
as startled plovers we turn at each hand
upon the doorway's sacking curtain, fear icing
to silence fragments of the unfinished tale.

A knitting factory, ten women shut in a room,
their wailing children, shut out, eat gutter scraps
while needles click, sound of forbidden speech,
click the clock's time, keeping time through Mao,
through temples become pigsties, the Cultural
Revolution, a cattle-prod up a monk's ass.
Her husband, a hundred miles of rock and ravine away,

bare handed, hoes potatoes, eyes sharp for
a gulp of worm, a lizard feast. As she speaks
my imagination freezes, can't move beyond
his bare hands in the dirt to the beating for eating
the lizard, although it thaws for shriveled cabbage
leaves, his friends peeled one by one by starvation's
pale, papery fingers, the glitter of cold's steel hand.

A ripple of blue roof tiles. At noon the servants
ate with her on a rug rampant with dragons.
Knitting, she and her maid share their Chinese rice gruel,
equality of hunger, while her son's
small arms and legs are wrung like dishcloths by bone
TB until Mao's hospital arrives.
"Mao must have lived in a town without a doctor," she says.

How does worm taste, I wonder as she tells
of hitching trucks to take her best wool *chuba*
to warm her husband, where frost cracks rocks.
Returning home she talks a driver out
of rape, sweating cold against the cab
door, "We're the same. We're both Tibetan. Don't."
Her laughter shivers into my shoulder.

Eighteen years. Mao dead. Her husband comes home
as foreigners bouncing in truck beds with wool bales, scratch
head lice, and tourists in shiny four-wheel drives
complain about service at the Holiday Inn.
Her restaurant feeds the transient world with whom
she speaks in the English she learned forty years
ago in a Darjeeling Anglican convent.

One night beneath a salting of stars, they roll
a rock away near what had been home and dig.
Light strikes her wedding jewelry, flashes coral,
turquoise, gold in a metal box. She matches
an Oslo girl's eyes with a loan of turquoise
earrings as Oslo marries London in Lhasa.
Coral bracelets reassume their rites on a stranger's wrist.

I take her dry hand in mine in the kitchen.
"I think we may be the same age," I say. "No."
I tell my age. "Oh," she says. "We Tibetans must have
done something very wicked." What could, should,
ought I to say to that or the flavor of worm or the nuns
in Dharmsala who, raped by the Chinese, have cloistered themselves
in the scent of pine against the unraped world.

On my sixth trip, passing through the sacking curtain
her waitress takes my hands and says, "She's dead.
Last year." We hold each other, while I feel
the emptiness open, the rail of the border-gate
rise on that vast unknown territory
of dry mountains naked in air, a finger
scrawl of path disappearing into distance.

I hand out small bills to red-robed monks, their tide
of chant rising and falling, dodging and dancing
between the bells and cymbals. I wonder where
she's reborn, Lagos, Alabama or closer? Will these
words find her, turn her toward the way, toward home?
But I see, through the butter lamp smoke, a path,
a dust scrawl, declining into distance.

THE DOG'S TOOTH OF FAITH

A traveling merchant's mother asked
him to bring her a Buddha relic.
On each trip he forgot, exchanging
news over *chang* with friends or flirting
with nomad girls in black tents, their
braids bright with turquoise beads or singing
love songs to mountain echoes as
he walked beside his loaded yaks.

The keeper of the family altar,
she changed the water bowls, filled butter
lamps where, with neighbors in a clutch
of houses, wind threw tantrums of dust.
She never scolded when he came
home, his bags filled with nothing but
silk, raisins, money, tea. He meant
to be a good son and felt sad.

Returning once from Lhasa he
remembered halfway home. While cursing
his thoughtlessness, he saw a dog's
jaw in the dust. He plucked a tooth
and wrapped it carefully in silk.
Her smiles broke her cheeks to the deep furrows
age had plowed into her face as
she set the tooth among the lamps.

Home from the next trip he, his eyes
adjusting to the darkness, stood
inside their door and watched resolve,
out of that dark, his mother, friends
in meditation there before
the tooth that through its silken wrapper
glowed incandescent rainbows. His
legs also folded to the lotus.

     Half-peeled potato in hand, Tashi says,
     "Faith makes even a dog's tooth shine rainbows."

THE VOYEURS

Lhasa lives inside a jaw snaggled
with the broken teeth of mountains.
Noon, Beijing Street is,
except for two policemen cramming rickshaws
with ruffled canopies into an alley,
empty for a breath before it's filled
by a siren's inexorable howl.

A white van, whose important passenger
wears khaki and gold braid, is followed by
a motorcycle phalanx with more braid
in sidecars. Finally the cause of this
parade in the beds of two baby-blue
Chinese trucks—in each, ten men, Tibetans,
are accompanied by Chinese soldiers.

In ironed uniforms, the soldiers stand, close
as Saturday night dates, beside their captives—
they'll execute them at the gutted temple
outside town. Now they force them to bow down
laying a gun on a back and leaning
or raising a pair of hands manacled
behind a back, so pain creates obeisance.

One not forced to bow has eyes spent as empty
cartridges—the world has disappeared.
Another, with a ripple of smile, looks
out, wolf-eyes ravening the mountains' rock.
Last glimpse of gold braid gone in a white car,
we gawkers at death and danger, queasy
with blood we've almost seen, go off to lunch.

THE BLIND DOG OF HOPE

Women make the barley leap in baskets outside
monastery gates. Dahlias in containers,
Chinese Army pork tins, petal afternoon,
overflowing purple blooms along the stair
leading from the temple's curtain to the court
where the German Shepherd with milky, blind eyes starts
at the young monk's voice that urges me to come in.

Showing the temple, he says six monks were taken
last month, no news—gone, disappeared—while the dog
listens to his voice, nose to tail, still as clay.
In the swept court, he commands those opaline
eyes in harsh Chinese, "Away." Tail down. Whole
body drooping with dejection. Then, "Come," sung
out in Tibetan, shivers joy down to the slapping
tail on court stones. So does the soul go dancing,
blind dog of despair, at the voice of hope's call.

TRANSPARENT GIRL

In the westering light,
her brother in a gold brocade cap
rocks gently on a loaded yak.
She, not much older, eight perhaps,

beside me on the path, a slight,
dark-eyed sprite layered in bright wools,
keeps pace awhile as she looks up,
face gravely tilting above her wraps.

Between our worlds, wings of star-dark space....
Outstripping my lowland pace she joins
the herded yaks, whose stomach noises
remind my ear of washing machines,

but turns from yak and kin to trace
steps back along the rock-strewn track
where peaks ghost the sky's growing dark.
Without a smile, severe, she leans

toward all that's alien to her nomad
life, points at my camera, at herself,
waits. At her dictate, I'm compelled;
I shutter her to transparency,

remove one girl forever clad
in this moment, while the other shouts a retort
to her swaying brother, perhaps the same report
the first one's silence speaks, "I'm here."

CIRCUMAMBULATING MOUNT KAILASH

The pass is well behind us now,
wind singing in its snows. We've wheeled
the mountain's hub along the brow
of riverbank, transgressions healed
by the circumference of our strides,
that circle us to a new birth.
But round this corner death's bromides
are laid out in their final dearth
beneath a long sheep-coat's gray curls.
A man and woman stand beside
this still heap, where the wind unfurls
a flag of dust. She's teary-eyed.
He's baffled, as if the hand he
grasped had gone empty as a glove.
The nomads and I, on the scree
path, pause in homage while we shove
hands into pockets and our packs.
We've been transformed to Magi, whose
gifts, yak cheese, candy, *tsampa,* stacks
of silvery coins, tumble loose
where death lies swaddled in its stone
bound manger, its young parents numb
in wind which, like death, has no bone
but molds another to become.

EPIPHANY IN A TENT

Aimless, I walk by the tent's black peak.

With an open hand, she gestures me in.
With my hand, I gesture fear of the mastiffs
galloping toward my strangeness, growling as though
they've rocks in their throats. She stones them to quiet.

The tent is booby-trapped with dirty cups,
a broken watch, and harnesses. We drink
tea sitting by the hearth and talk by hands,
by my measly hoard of Tibetan words.
By touch, we discourse through the other's things.

Gold-brocade new hat with earflaps, the two
lenses of my camera, her coral
ring, my green eyes become our conversation.
There's a ruckus outside of snorts and barks.
She knows, leaps out of the tent into the sounds.

Waiting in the open folds of the tent,
wearing it, a huge skirt billowing
black behind me, I look to the vast
treeless, green lap of her world that moves
with animals in the custody of mountains.

She returns, asks, using sun and road,
when I'll leave tomorrow.
                Morning,
out the Cruiser's window, woman, tent,
dark against horizon's rising fire.
I raise my hand.

A PILGRIM INTO SILENCE

The road forks left where we stop on the wind-
scoured edge of ridge; I don't remember why.
Below me glitters the spread of a sere, saltlick
plain cordoned off by ranks of mountains in
soft mineral pastels above which white's
finality is slouching in its shroud.
What little is alive knows to clutch the earth—
a web of green set with gust-tremored blooms
like lattices of sea-foam sliding over
humped backs of waves. Always I've thought it would
be like this—naked rock sharp under sun,
wind singing, sprung steel of a rapier
in my ears. I take the dust blown fork, walk
to emptiness, a pilgrim into silence.

THE RAVEN

Here, where killing is forbidden, antelope,
legs delicate as wishbones, spring the stone
block scarp of Kailash, the sacred mountain's slope.

I watch them, fragile against the rock like blown,
downy seed. Below me, somewhere, a bird shrieks,
terror desperate in its wordless tone.

A man, with glee at his dexterity,
is twirling, by the monastery wall,
a raven, swinging it at arm's length by the feet.

Wings waver wildly for balance, skeet target,
live clay bird, a screaming prisoner
on its dizzy wheel of human cleverness.

Home

THE CROW'S OBITUARY FOR THE DORSET HOTEL

Crows glide on wing-tip shine
into deconstructed hotel rooms
their ceilings shorn, wall half dismantled,
these chambers indecently exposed
by sun as a blousy archeology
of paints' exfoliate colors,
intestinal snarls of wire and pipes.

Winging down in the rainbow oil
slick of their mourning suits, these drifters,
among jack-hammers jettisoned
till Monday, once could only strut
the terraces, but now they bounce
between unlidded rooms. They are
in possession and browse solemnly
as funeral directors pricing
cemetery plots. Without
a caw, they lift on requiem wings.

BIGAMY

The cultural bigamist hitches from Lhasa on the Madison
Avenue bus, to tea and talk over scones
and Devonshire cream, or is it dried strips of mutton
with two truck drivers and pantomime speech that roams
through fingers warmed by yak butter tea dispensed
from a Chinese thermos, Chippendale chairs or a lichened
rock. On the monastery court's reverenced
stones, monklets cover her from the balcony's bend
with plastic uzis and ten year old grins.
She mutates them to angels, boy sopranos
in a basket, hovering song above the chagrin
of Papageno's chimes. Is she grandiose
believing she's got two worlds on a string,
does she have neither by mutual forfeiting?

GULMIT, PAKISTAN / NEW YORK, SEPT. 11, 2001

Corralled within the snow-lapped peaks,
a barrier to all airwaves
that circulate the world's feats and fears,
the houses nestle inside their walls
in half-harvested potato fields—
a web of family and neighbor.

On the globe's far side, down the corridor
of hours, a friend watched at her window,
the sidewalks full, a steady pour
of people moving north; the cars,
a solid current, obeyed the meter
of lights, no voice, no horn—a moving silence.

In mountains, where violence may inhabit
the next valley, a man said,
"We're a peaceful people." His niece held on
to his smallest finger. "What will become of us?"
His glance moved to mountains
that would not let the news through.

On my return a friend subdues
her hair with one hand, telling me
that amid the shattered glass on her rug,
in a room which once had amazing views,
she found a pair of men's brown shoes,
polished, laced, and neatly tied.

STREET SCENE

She is walking toward me on Fifty-fourth Street,
slim, young, in black, the shade New York's chic count on,
a lovely stride of knees sheathed in black nylon
above spike heels firm on the sidewalk's concrete.
Suddenly her hands rise to her cheeks as she weeps,
body bent as though by a blow, hair drawn,
wings across her face against the neon
and eyes of the city. The collapse of defeat
drops her, a songbird's plummet through the air.
Eyes averted, I pass, see beyond her his straight
back, a furled umbrella cased in a suit without a sigh.
But I must not judge. Perhaps he's had an escape
from need or greed or a mind sweet and silly as Jell-O.
It was just the collapse, the suddenness of her sorrow.

NEIGHBORHOOD REVENANT

He dwelt beneath the stoop and carved acanthus
of the vacant townhouse down the block. A revenant
of reality on a prosperous street, a key-
less inhabitant, who Saturdays scrubbed
his den with Lysol, Clorox, until one day
new owners padlocked his home where Central Park
carriage horses woke him walking through his nights.

Evicted, he returns, sits beside the stoop
with books, and notepads, a pretense of a life
whose stolen, lost or abandoned contents have
long since been swirled away on some dark spurn
of wave to leave the wiry coat hanger
of a black man in artist's black accessorized
with a ski mask bandaging his mouth,
censored by the leisure of poverty.

After eight years we say good morning, his Natchez
drawl embellishing those words with a courtliness
that makes me feel graced, my day more luminous.
One autumn night, when torches of gingkoes flared
the street, on the grating of the University Club,
where light seeped up from the basement, I saw him
an illumination of soles, as he tapped in the night,
soft shoe among the year's nub of yellow leaves.

FIFTH AVENUE

On the west, trees fringe the Avenue with green.
On the east, the buildings line up, a gray militia.
Down the center cruise lemon lozenge
taxis through the summer air as lazy
as a slow blues bass line. Polar bears lie
on their heaps of melting ice cubes, monkeys doze,
the seal slips round and round her rocky island.

I'm in first love again, ten, scurrying
to dance, piano class; my eyes are moons bigger
than my mind, a greedy shine of admiring envy
that wants just everything from snake-skin shoes
to that woman's life, the one in the asymmetric
hat flipped up over her precise brunette
curls and a drop pearl earring's swing and sway.

I'm still sure her life's more exciting, though
I live here now, own an asymmetric hat,
don't travel homeward watching the lights from the train's
soot-streaked windows, the lights—those framed candles
of lives, the stories I still desire.
The park-seal flips moonlit flanks to slow-
plucked blues, slips round and round her rocky island.

SWEET REVEILLE ON 54TH ST.

A ricochet of trumpet
skims its water-strider of sound across
dawn light on curtained glass
walls of my canyon. Leaning from
my morning window, I
can't see him, but the glancing notes
dance on all surfaces
to make a ballroom of our building
cliffs with glissading phrases.
Now I can see the silver gleam
of horn. A Gabriel
upon a low roof, at an imagined
corner of the round
world, he blows into the ripening
blush of a New York summer
morning, trumpets *Body and Soul.*

I'd arrived in foolish shoes. She lent me sneakers,
size ten. "Too large for you," she said. Barn red.
I shuffled in them. "Do you think I'm dying?"
she asked. "Yes," I replied. "Anyway, return
them," she said. "You don't really know."
But I did know, and, damn it, I was right.

We were two women for whom life was to write.
Jew / Catholic. Head / Tail. A pair of sneakers
in the male domain. The only red my childhood knew
was my hair, while in Chicago she was raised Red
and Orthodox. We broke out of our religions
into life like ex-cons hell-bent against that kind of dying.

I wedded a louche lush, had a marriage dying
from its first day. She married Ernie, the right
man, older, a statistician who, when they returned
from China, lived uptown, while she moved her sneakers
to the Village. By accident one day she read
another woman's letter to him. She never asked or knew.

Did she sleep with him? I never had the nerve to ask.
She loved him. In his weeks of dying
she was at the hospital on red
alert and shocked the doctors demanding her right
to photograph his dead face, no sneaker
she. In profile, he hung on her wall, her return

to the man who, whatever she'd done or hadn't, did not turn
from her. Whatever the agreement, they'd kept it. No
sex, perhaps, but fidelity. Long hair and sneakers,
after cancer, short hair, among the literati of the dying
century, barely capable of right or write,
and certainly bleeding slowly all the red

from their souls. She mourned, I think, the bright Red
certainty of childhood to whose hopes she could not return
and the sister whose choice she wept right
to the crushed goblet. "How could she marry him. He knew
nothing," she said. "His brains were dead, not dying.
To sound sharp, he'd parrot other people, the sneak."

On the day, I brought back the sneakers, the pair, red
as the sickle's background, not knowing she died.
But she had, after all, the right of return.

232 FARRINGDON RD.

Soft ball of bloom, the last pink rose
against the neighbor wall in the garden
will molt its petals to amen
on any itinerant draft's slight blows.

The BBC is calm among oxalis
leaves shivered by the mating foxes' yarr,
a shrill in love's vernacular
that rends the sonatina's artifice.

Geranium petals blown in through
the second story window leave
their blood gouts on the old gray weave
of rug in a child's room residue.

Top floor, the betrayed bed sleeps one on
one side. Beyond the pane, a magnolia's bower,
whose stiff leaves nest one final flower
gone brown, an old tea stain on linen.

SHAKESPEARE

Steel subway wheels grind out tormented shrieks.
An Asian elf—between dark waterfalls
of hair, a lotus-pale face—she shouts across
the bodies swaying in their winter coats,
"An expense of spirit in a waste of shame...."
Caucasian, braces stapling his smile, he
removes his earphones, gives her a spaniel stare,
"Macbeth?" he ventures. "No, no, no, the sonnets."
Now recognizing it's a game, he struggles
a moment. "Get thee to a nunnery,"
he hurls among strap-hanging shopping bags
and newspapers. "That's *Hamlet,"* she returns
crisp as a snapped bean. "This royal throne
of kings, this scept'red isle, this earth of majesty,
this seat of Mars," each word is savored
on her tongue with passion as a smile folds her
eyes closed. He's fogged behind the swaying scrim
of riders. "That's John of Gaunt's death speech
in *King Richard II,"* I pounce and crash their party.
Each ion of my professor's soul is quivering—
the antennae vibe of some obscure subspecies
that's homing in on its own. "Ripeness is all,"
I throw into the corridor that's thick
with bodies. *"Lear,"* she trills triumphant. "Let
me not to ... something ... to the marriage
of true minds," he stumbles in, dead set on tracking
her through this topiary maze of tripping tongue.
I rise at Union Square on battered, 500-year-old rhymes,
aches of archaic song as on a kite's wind-swirl
of tail or the painted bulb of a hot air balloon.
The heirs are apparent; who would not die happy?

A MEDITATION ON ADOLESCENCE

—For Rhys and Ethan Andersen

Consider the flounder one day discerning
that one of his eyes has unmoored and gone touring
to join up with its partner, which is not reassuring,
however much parents may talk of maturing.

Now his vision's one-sided, his body is flat,
he may look like his father but his *caveat*
is he wished to be sleek like a hake or a sprat
when prepared for the human commissariat.

Or imagine you're the albatross fuzzy and weak,
long after blue boobies have adult physique.
Your parents arrive, barf down your beak,
and mumble vague lessons about flight technique.

Unflappable on ground, twelve foot wings for levitation
must be run off the cliff-edge where waves beat percussion
below gull-crying rocks at a thousand foot elevation.
You must trust wind will hold you upon its exultation.

GYPSY ROSE LEE

Plucking off her elbow-length black gloves
slowly, a finger at a time—piccolo,
piccolo—she was a syncopated confusion
of my childhood, a lady who took off her clothes.
A girl friend leafing through *Life* asked, "How could
she in front of her parents?" While another girl
searched for stray pubic hairs on a View Master slide.
I scanned her face for the hallmarks mother'd taught
me to distinguish vulgar from refined.
Years later, mother's spectrum firmly mastered
common to genteel, I saw her headed toward death
on TV in a plunging velvet gown, off mother's
scale, and, for me forever, an air on a G string.

HOW MANY MOTHERS

I

does one have? The one before you're born
you only know in echoes.

Old letters, her death left
among bent snapshots of unknown
men in World War One khakis,
are dizzy still, some seventy
years later, with her bliss
at being beyond the rules, as if
she stood outside in thunderous
air grasping her risk, charged with joy.

She stayed alone three months in Tunis,
wrote, "At Ramadan's
end the *Bey* walks the *souks* attended
by courtiers in their flashing
silks, shadowed velvets, and the glint
of golden dagger hilts.
Men pressed against the stalls cheer—waves
that swell before, die after."

II

The one that I believe I knew
for forty years, is she
more real than her precursor was?

The one hysterical
with rage, the one intimidated
by Princeton graduates,
the one who, when I had measles,
read me *Kidnapped* and *Kim*
but only traveled in

the big-sky summers through
seas of wheat to her Fargo aunts.

I match these with the backhand
that broke my nose, the lash of tongue
and dog-chain— "Stupid. Dumb.
You haven't got the sense God gave
a goose. You'll marry, never
hold a job." She taught me New York.
At nine, let me loose as
an elver on its avenues.

III

That one's dead. The last lives inside
me till I die, shape-shifter,
the shadow-mother of my mind.

Her letters reveling
in risk I jigsaw with the wife
who told me "Never marry,"
the grandma gleeful at her grandson's
pissed waterfall down garden
stairs; she let me piss down stairs, never.
She made me bloomers, made
me sit on the top stair while she

looked up at their lace edges
at what she thought was wanted from
a girl of five. The nose
that's broken in my mirror has
been reimbursed by the right
she gave my roamings
in Thailand and Tibet. I'm her
urn of ashed memory.
All these mothers die with me.

DRIVING

There were no licenses when she learned to drive,
just straight dirt roads between green fields of wheat
that bent to her wind, which spurned with its passing heat
the ripe green heads and made the rabbits dive
into the thicket of swaying stalks. It was
her way to delete her mother, the world. Once wed
she drove away from arguments, buried
them in the speed of her anger, which became both cause
and effect. When she picked up the hitchhiker Death,
that beggar's first demand was the alms of her eyes,
the cataracts were the blur of his breath,
his exhale shrinking her boundaries without reprise.
He shut her highways, lowered his border bar,
till the only way out was on his road, in his car.

A GIRL GOES INTO THE WORLD

... but
Mother called me back
from the end of the sandy drive:
"It's different for girls."

—*Jane Kenyon,* "A Boy Goes into the World"

Never did she say, "It's different for girls,"
not even when in fear she called the police
while I, lost in the forest, picked a way
through blackberry brambles, hearing conversations
of last year's whispering dead beneath my feet
with the living in the wind above my head,
unaware that I should be afraid,
until I came to a road I knew and a neighbor
who'd been sent out in her car to patrol and find me.
She wasn't even angry. She knew the price.
And yes, she knew it was a lie, her pretense
that a girl could safely have a boy's adventure.
But, I believed. And so I bless her lie.
Bless her. Bless the lie that blessed me.

SILENT LIVES

Riding through rowan trees, red berries
bright as vengeance blood, air loud with the litter
of leaves beneath the horses' hooves, we move,
walkers and riders alone, aloof in our thoughts
contained in our bone kingdom of skull, that nation
of the solitary with no intruders, the terminus
in our silent lives, so that never can we completely
be in a strange land even trotting in Bhutan
or walking beneath the spattered blood of the rowans
but always we're resident in two countries, our own
and the exterior nation—when the one goes dark
we will no longer be able to see the other—
but for now, in Bhutan, on horse and foot,
we journey in our company of sole by sole.

WHAT WOMAN HAS A COUNTRY?

What woman has a country? Always she's
the alien in a male nation, papers
disheveled, visa date blurred, her strategies
for sanctuary require that she barter
self for place within the borders or else, misfit,
illegal, grow lean upon her loneliness,
a susurrus of shadow at the limits.
Where has she journeyed from, she dispossessed
of all hands hold, companioned only by
the fair wind of memory. In desert quiet
a windmill's piston creaks to prophecy
the small cry of water in the dust, or the duet
of a raven echoing its matinal
voice and shadow on river, on canyon wall.

About the Author

Born in New York City, Karen Swenson was raised in the suburb of Chappaqua and went to Barnard College. She received her MA from NYU. She has been published by *The New Yorker* and many small literary magazines, as well as *Saturday Review.* Her travel articles have appeared in *The New York Times* and *The Wall St. Journal.* She has traveled for two months of each year in SE Asia for the last 27 years. She presently teaches at NYU and Barnard.